LOVE STORY

LOVE STORY

Heaven's Orchestrated Melody of Love

LYKOURGOS TZAKIS

RESOURCE *Publications* • Eugene, Oregon

LOVE STORY
Heaven's Orchestrated Melody of Love

Copyright © 2025 Lykourgos Tzakis. All rights reserved. Except for brief quotations in critical publications or reviews, no part of this book may be reproduced in any manner without prior written permission from the publisher. Write: Permissions, Wipf and Stock Publishers, 199 W. 8th Ave., Suite 3, Eugene, OR 97401.

Resource Publications
An Imprint of Wipf and Stock Publishers
199 W. 8th Ave., Suite 3
Eugene, OR 97401

www.wipfandstock.com

PAPERBACK ISBN: 979-8-3852-4074-6
HARDCOVER ISBN: 979-8-3852-4075-3
EBOOK ISBN: 979-8-3852-4076-0
VERSION NUMBER 01/08/25

This book contains real life experiences and events, therefore all second & third party names and photos of all facial images have not been made manifest in the pages of this here book in all respect for private security reasons.

I dedicate this book to *my beloved lady*,
the love of my life.

> Take a flower and
> set it beside your
> heart and in time
> it will fade away.
> Take my love and
> set it inside your
> heart and it will
> live forever.

You may be anonymous in this here book,
but your name is signed across my heart.

This book is not about "us, and by the way God also." This book is about loving, caring God with us. God is much bigger than our story, our experiences, and even our failures.

Knowing and living The Truth qualifies me to write about the truth, for love does not need permission to act, and I do not need permission to love.

Contents

Prologue | *ix*

Chapter 1 Once Upon a Time… | 1
Chapter 2 Gods law VS mans tradition | 11
Chapter 3 God's Providence | 17
Chapter 4 Law VS Grace | 24
Chapter 5 Not called to do, but to trust Him | 34
Chapter 6 Love by chance, stay by choice | 42
Chapter 7 Money, matters! | 53

Epilogue | 59

About the Author | 61

Prologue

THIS BOOK DESCRIBES A true romantic love story in a poetic way between a man and a woman with different religious and social backgrounds, living on two different continents where they both started out as business colleagues and friends and later fell in love with each other, and at the appointed time were united by God. Second this book is a testimony describing God's providence which the couple experienced, with precise dates. Though we tend to focus on the miraculous, of course God can do everything He wants, but God most often works through providence, rather than the miraculous. God's providence in our daily lives is the idea that God takes natural events, and He enacts supernatural results. Things happen everyday in life, and God uses all those things to work out a supernatural outcome. Therefore God can take/use anything that happens to us, it's not an impediment to Him, it's never a *"oh, no what am I going to do now?"* moment for God.

> Romans 8:28 *And we know that all things work together for good to them that love God, to them who are the called according to his purpose.*

This book is written on a fresh basis of multiple scriptural teachings infused with everyday life in mind, and focuses on the subject of *"marriage"* as the main theme, teaching all people by putting in the true prospective and based on the the true meaning of the Greek word in the Bible for marriage which is "Γάμος" – pronounced (Gamos) explaining the difference between mans traditional marriage protocol and the Marriage contract before

Prologue

God, with scriptural proof and knowledge, with live examples and testimonies, an up to date study of the truth and knowledge about *"marriage"* and our responsibility before God, based on our sincere motivations.

This book was written to teach and comfort, and give hope to all people, that God is love and loves us all the same despite our different denominations, and theories. God is one, that listens and really cares for us all and our well being. God is all knowing and everywhere and in all things, He is the ancient of days and knows perfectly how things operate including all of us as individuals and as a whole, therefore this book is also about trusting God to choose for us what is the best, because He is perfect, thus putting mans tradition in an acceptable time and place but not above God's law while maintaining a good solid relationship with God through *"knowing"* Jesus Christ and placing religion in its rightful place which is . . . *"NO WHERE!"* Christianity is not a set of rules we follow and everything is fine, it is a relationship with Jesus Christ.

My goal is to inform people correctly and help sharpen their conscience and their ability to tell right from wrong, concerning the truth about the *"marriage contract"* before God, to help today's and tomorrow's youth make a sincere choice based on the facts of scripture rather on mans traditional point of view, of this sensitive subject people touch only on the surface, if at all. The fact is that if you do not break any eggs, you can not eat an omelet.

This book should be given as instruction to young adults mature and seeking love, however the meat material contained is not easy for everyone to chew on, rather some *milk drinkers* might not easily chew and digest its content, and could very well set it aside or even lightly pass it by.

I strongly advise teachers of Scripture that have this book in their possession to *"chew and digest first themselves"* before serving to others.

We can grow as much as we want

Chapter 1

Once Upon a Time...

ONCE UPON A TIME, is how this unique love story begins, I believe everyone loves a good love story especially one with a happy ending. Since the start of human storytelling history, humans have enjoyed great romance stories from Romeo and Juliet, Cleopatra and Mark Antony to Paris and Helen of Troy. Our story may be different or less significant as a celebrity, but also important with its unique challenges, and obstacles, as every other couple in love.

After my ex-wife divorced me, due to financial problems on 28/03/2016, for many years after that and numerous disappointments I started thinking a bit negative, that I was meant to be alone from here on after in this life, and happiness to be with someone special was forever gone from me. I had a wall built around me and my defense was as a stronghold to protect myself from all the relationships that have come and gone over the years. None of the women I interacted with met my criteria or arouse my senses for that matter. Worse off I saw that people will only try to take advantage of you if you open the door for them to do so, I said to my heart be strong, be independent, as time went by and my relationship with God grew better my heart grew soft, compassionate, supporting and loving people unconditionally expecting nothing in return, I gave the love I never had basically. Business was going bad, global economy was terrible and I could not afford to waste time and money on relationships, however no matter what I did, work, ministry, music I could not shake the feeling that I was alone and especially during and around the Hollidays, I was desperate to feel alive again, to feel the warm companionship of a woman, I wanted to be loved for who I am and not to be looked at as an ATM machine, and despite the bad financial circumstances, I was deep inside my heart and soul searching endlessly for that perfect woman that will fill my gap, up until God's providence knitted circumstances together for a special person of His perfect choosing and timing to walk into my life and made my hearts desire a reality.

I was regularly on Sunday morning attending a local non-denominational congregation, the preaching was in English and when people visited Belgrade from around the world they were welcome to come and worship with us, and because of the freedom we offered people from other denominations came and local people as well. We were not a big group but we were a warm group and they made every effort to make me family, home away from home, as a matter of fact in my difficult moments they were always eager to extend a helping hand. Like every congregation we had external activities that I would go to as a member, like prayer meetings and Bible studies, I was hungry for God and I desperately tried very hard to learn all I can about Him and His will for me, I was looking for wisdom, knowledge and understanding as well as guidance.

God always knows exactly where we are in our journey of faith and precisely what it will take to get our attention, because He wants to lead and guide us into the destiny into the wonderful future He has planned for us, but often we are simply not listening, and God needs to get our attention and often requires something out of the ordinary, but it may not be spectacular, or pleasant. It may hurt us, or challenge us, or cause anxiety, but no matter the method, God will use whatever He thinks it takes to get our attention, because He loves us!

On September 15, 2021, it was a Wednesday evening and after concluding our mens Bible study, we were at the time studying the book of Acts at a brothers in Christ house, and one of the leaders of our congregation was asking if there were any prayer requests, I

Once Upon a Time...

raised my hand first (I was feeling very lonely after six years without a touch of a woman) and asked to pray for God to give me a virtuous woman (Proverbs 31:10) to marry, as I was seeking companionship and could not find any that could measure up to what I needed at the time, so the leader responded *"okay we will pray for a good Christian woman for you"* and I responded *"no, please pray for a God fearing woman for me"*, for a Christian woman was a too much of a general term in our days, and all present thought this was a logical request and so we all bowed our heads and agreed in the prayer and intersession was made for me.

On September 22, 2021 I was doing my own Bible study (continuing on the book of Acts) at home and that because our mens Bible study was a bit disorganized, too much interactivity and no study plan was set or printed out, so discussions among people with dissimilar levels of biblical understanding was a bit problematic. Beginners felt overwhelmed when the discussion gets into deeper waters. Those with more knowledge sometimes got frustrated by the "shallow" questions beginners typically have and the basic answers which must follow. Then the study became a discussion with quotes such as *"I feel this is . . .*", or *"I believe this is . . ."* and not the usual Bible quotes as example: *"scripture says in John chapter one verse three"*, no cross-referencing, nothing of the sort, so it was a great mens get together for coffee, tea, cookies and sandwiches, a great time I might say for relationships, but that is not what I was spiritually hungry for, so I politely complained to the leadership and was ignored at first then they tried to organize somehow but with no foundation the structure fell, and so I quietly separated my self from the mens Bible study that was held in various peoples houses and started digging into scripture on my own, unaware of God's Devine loving plan.

I was on (Acts 10:1–48), this is where Peter got a vision from God and was taught that he should not call common or unclean what God cleansed, God was making an example using food, for Peter was hungry at the time. This was God's introduction to get his attention to go and talk to Cornelius the Roman centurion and to preach to him (the gentile) that feared God, the gospel of Christ so he can be saved, and so Peter finally after the third time did as he was told and Cornelius and his household those who listened were saved, and the Holy Spirit came upon them.

The very next day on September 23, 2021 in the afternoon, I get a call from an old friend and colleague of mine a woman I knew for eight (8) years from Jakarta Indonesia: Today known and written in this book as *my beloved lady*. Many years ago we collaborated on different oil and gas projects together from time to time, we also established a company together in Jakarta Indonesia with a couple of other partners, but it did not work out properly, so because we had only expenses and no income we agreed to close it down. *My beloved lady* and I, though we had not spoken to each other for about six (6) years, due to our different busy schedules, on that particular evening she had in her heart to call me because she wanted to present her new financial project to me, I was happy to hear her voice again for I always was intrigued by the way she was a fighter, that never gave up, and I was so happy that she remembered me, and then all of a sudden something stirred me up inside so much so I could not think about business, so I asked her a simple honest question from the bottom of my heart, for I considered her always to be a good friend so I had the confidence to speak to her openly, for my intention was for her to introduce a female friend of hers, to me.

"*Where can I find a beautiful woman like you that is also compatible as you are to me, and single to marry? Do you have any friends that are single?*"

She was caught by surprise with this question, and was amazed I considered her beautiful, and I told her I always thought she was beautiful, and her response was; "*What about me?*" I was intrigued by her, so I responded boldly without any doubt by saying "*I am interested,*" then she asked me concerning my marriage, I explained to her how my ex-wife gave me a divorce so I was no longer married and I was looking for a companion. She then confided in me that she was now a widow and was available and also praying and looking for a man, also with her late husband they were many years separated because he cheated on her with another woman. She confided in me and said that she always liked me, and respected me, when she was separated at the time she even prayed to God for us to be together, and I was like "*WOW!*", one kind word here one compliment there, one simple loving gesture led to another and just like that we both fell in love.

It was crystal clear to me that it was God's intervention, God working behind the scenes His providence which was not apparent but manifested at the perfect time, it was His will, that enacted through the natural world, it was His loving kindness and care that combined us together and despite our religious differences, me being a Christian (a follower of Christ) and her being a muslim. We can see of two times in the whole Bible God did tell someone whom to marry, (Hosea 1:2 and Matthew 1:20–21) so it is also Biblical. The fact is that God is love not religion and God loves us all the same despite our different denominational differences, God looks in the heart and *my beloved lady* has a good and sensitive heart, a beautiful God fearing woman, honest, sincere and 100% compatible with me, born on November 04 1970 three (3) years younger than me, with all the qualities I was praying about in a woman, perfect match!

My beloved lady was a dynamic business woman, smart with strong identity and well connected on a global scale, she was into banking, mining, frozen fish, chicken slaughter house and a very famous supplier of safety wear to the government, her family also owned once a small bank too.

I always admired her for her strength and her dedication to her work. As a woman she was very beautiful with a perfect thin figure and her love made me feel alive and young again, when I looked into her inviting warm eyes I felt her acceptance and embracement, when hearing her voice I felt her respect, I had value, her smile was so enchanting that melted my heart like butter, for the first time and for a very long time I felt I was not alone anymore, her presence (though we were video chatting on line) filled me and gave me hope, I felt that I had obtained favor with God and I finally found my soul mate, I felt lighter than air, and I just wanted to open wings and fly . . . preferably in her arms.

Her love brought out the best in me, in a way that the hope of another person caring for me made me want to live not just exist, for instance I used to cut my hair very short and because she said that I look better with longer hair I changed my hair style to longer and combing it a side rather than my head looking like a tennis ball. She also made some comments concerning my weight and she was right so she set a goal for me to lose five kilos, and she prescribed a program to remove some bad habits of mine, like sodas, potato chips, and too much sugar, to regularly exercise and keep fit, so I was motivated to actually start doing some of that on a regular basis, and to be honest I felt good losing those extra kilos. There was this one time that I called her to confess my so called sin to her and she asked what did I do and I was holding a bag of potato chips and just as she saw what I meant she started to laugh, I just love to make her laugh, as she was even more beautiful, her face lights up like a neon sign, bursting with joy from deep within, and of course I was forgiven.

There was this other time she was talking to me about her religious regime that it was strict and how women rights were neglected and she went into a conversation that was quite sad but I listened to her, and when the conversation started to get a bit depressing, I politely and spontaneously moved in changing the subject to cheer her up with a joke, I said to her that my regime is much more strict that yours, and she was a bit surprised in her mind thinking I meant Christianity, so she asked me: "*How is your regime more strict than mine?*" Then I said this to her: "*well my regime says that I have to lose ten kilos, not eat potato chips and soda and not to much sugar.*" She then burst into laughter and she said to me: "*yes you are right your regime is more strict.*" We both laughed and positivity filled the air once more as our spirits were up, then she said with a cute positive tone in her voice: "*I am your regime*" then I replied to her: "*I love you my regime,*" she then responded with a cute dictator type of manor with her index finger pointing at me: "*and your regime says stick to your diet.*" She then told me that she was proud of me for being a hard and persistent worker, and that she loved me and wanted to be with me, and every time she was a little warm with me, not a lot, just a little spark was enough to light me on fire.

    I was in love with her and I wanted to be with her, I knew and *with out a single doubt* that God was with us, I was filled with righteousness peace and joy, so letting peace in my heart, soul and mind make the decision out of faith and love on September 25, 2021 I asked her to marry me and she gladly accepted, she said "*yes*" with joy in her heart, where this was our first verbal commitment before God, and from then on she became an intimate part of my life. *My beloved lady* confided in me that she loved me for quite some time now, as a matter of fact she told me that she was waiting for me for eight years, "talk about patience," she also confided in me that God had done a great change in my character, eight years ago I was cold and distant, business focused and strict, where now she sees a warm hearted, loving considerate and sensitive for the feelings of others, and a *humble person*, that loves God, as a matter of fact when she called me that afternoon on account of my "*new improved*" response, *she thought she called the wrong number*. That confession is the change that God had worked in me all these years, the Lord had been sanding down all the rough edges of my character into the likeness of His image, and that took time, and mutual collaboration. So I sought a way to go to her and ask her hand in marriage officially, for I was at the time situated in Belgrade Serbia and she was in Jakarta Indonesia, plus my financial situation was not at its best at the time. She became my motivation for a greater level of success and I pursued to make things happen to go to her while simultaneously God worked with us, in us and through us to secure a future for He loves and cares for us. Though we were both in love we still had a lot to learn about each-other, now closer than before with an open channel of intimacy and communication things were different than the friendship we had before, now love was taking over, and familiar feelings and emotions sprung up, hidden or compressed, from both sides that we had to deal with, throw away and make room for a new thing that God was doing in our lives, feelings that we both needed deliverance from and time for healing.

A foundation is placed on a rock to hold steady a house, business, relationships, life itself. If we build any foundation on, business and money, fame and power, passion, then our foundation is sand, and when these elements disappear everything around us starts to sink. If we build on Love (1 Corinthians 13) then our foundation is rock solid and even with passion gone, the foundation still stands in time and endures every storm. Every work is tried with fire and all our work is shown for what it is, when brought to light. It is revealed with fire, and the fire will test the quality of each person's work. If what has been built survives, the builder will receive a reward, the reward is that which remains, if it is burned up, consumed, the builder will suffer loss. We both went through various disappointments in business, but that only made us stronger as individuals, and more organized, however the pressures and delays of all business ventures we were involved in manifest the priorities we had and simultaneously revealed what sort of vessels we are, simultaneously freeing us from our past emotional traumas, its just that sometimes time is all that we need to properly connect, and our hearts to be set right by the Master Tuner.

I love her and I know in my heart she loves me, we both long to meet and be together one day, surely under God's perfect loving circumstances, with our past emotional traumas and money not being any issue, therefore we wait upon the Lord, that united us to finish His work, for it is easy to get married but we need to have the right set up, (emotional & Financial) to stay married.

Love to be true love is always vulnerable, Jesus put His heart on the line as someone would do anytime someone loves somebody. To love at all in any capacity is to feel pain, is to hurt. When we engage in marriage we engage an ideal person, but when we marry we marry a real person. We discover each others humanity and every relationship is like that, we have to be vulnerable to love. We need to make a choice either we can tear up the picture of the image of the person we are carrying around with us and love and accept the real person in front of us, or tear up the real person and love the image we cary around with us.

God is in full control and there is no need to to worry, only prayer, and supplication making known to God all things. The difference between the truth and a lie is that the lie does not bear any fruit, on the other hand the truth, given some time it produces fruit.

Your will gives power and life

Chapter 2

Gods law VS mans tradition

> Mark 7:7-13 *Howbeit in vain do they worship me, Teaching for doctrines the commandments of men. For laying aside the commandment of God, ye hold the tradition of men, ... And he said unto them, Full well ye reject the commandment of God, that ye may keep your own tradition.*

THE ENGLISH WORD "MARRIAGE" derives from a 13th century French word and is a bit misleading as to its roots. The event of marriage today and since ancient times is managed and directed in every society, in compliance with certain rules and patterns conforming to their pattern of culture, that has been executing the traditional event-ritual of marriage. However exiting and fun all this is and sounds, mans tradition is not the word of God, and we are not married because of any protocol or man made law or tradition when we enter a building and someone says "*I now pronounce you husband and wife, you may kiss the bride*", or when we sign a legal government document, "*NO*" not so! And unfortunately traditionalism seeks to uphold these traditions and is resistant to change, which is fine, we all love tradition but it is not the "*marriage contract*" before God, people are misinformed.

Weather we know, practice it, or not, we all have the same access to God through Jesus Christ, Jesus Christ alone is the only eternal priest, and is accessible by everyone that seeks Him, this is fact, because Jesus is truly risen.

I have a very good friend that I respect also a Christian, that has helped me numerous times both emotionally and financially, my friend and brother has had multiple sexual relations with other women, looking for the perfect companion, unlike me that was seeking and waiting upon God for seven years to reveal someone to me, (not judging my friend and beloved brother), though I believe he did ask God deep in his heart but was not patient enough to wait on God to reveal to him the perfect spouse and on his own he tries to find the right one, and in his heart once he finds her he stated that: "*I will get married in church.*" Now this response sounds like something normal and a couple of years ago I would pass it by as something normal. My friend did not mean a traditional wedding he meant it exactly as it sounds: "*I will get married in church*" as if to say the marriage contract before God is done in the church, meaning because of the ritual being conducted. Now as scriptural knowledge and understanding has kicked in my system like a hot cup of coffee in the morning waking me up I can safely say; People Wake Up and smell the coffee!

First of all nowhere in the New Testament is there any Biblical Command for the marriage ritual to be in a Church Building. Second and most important all these things we think we know is not what God had intended for a marriage to be like, and this mentality, this thinking is everywhere, lack of fear of God due to global religious stupidity, and I too was guilty of the same, why? Because nobody is taking the time to talk about marriage or teach this subject properly, with the same meaning that God has intended it to have, rather we are following a traditional path, already prepared for us and not questioning anything, because most of us it suits us just fine, not knowing, only to continue in our comfortable and pleasurable path, of self righteousness.

Make no mistake I am not against our traditions or am I apposed to our governing law of registered marriage, I am in favor of both and so is Jesus (John 2:1–12). I am merely explaining in an analysis the Greek word for marriage that is recorded in the New Testament which is ΓΑΜΟΣ – and pronounced (Gamos). So as we analyze and accept the Greek word AGAPI for what it means, then we must equally accept and analyze the Greek word *Gamos* and what it means, which is a combining form meaning "*joined, united,*" "*joining, union,*" used in the formation of compound words, such as "γαμέβομαι" pronounced (gamevome) meaning I am being married. The Greek Word *Gàmos* (Γάμος) politely describing the word which means "*the marriage,*" however the vulgar word *Gamò* (Γαμώ) spelled-pronounced differently describes "*the action marriage*" also known as (sex), both similar meaning with same roots but different usage. Marriage is NOT a sacrament-mystery of the church, the word comes from the verb (gameo–mo–gamevome) "γαμεω–μω–γαμευομαι" and it has nothing to do with religion but with the union of two people. Therefore if God deliberately knitted together history for the New Testament to be written in the Greek language using Alexander the Great to begin spreading it, and after his successors maintaining it, thus expressing His perfect meaning of each and every word, then we too must be educated and aware to have the same meaning as Him.

> Matthew 19:3-5 *The Pharisees also came unto Him, tempting Him, and saying unto Him* . . .

Why do you think the Pharisees came with this specific question to tempt Him? Simply because divorce was a common problem back then as it is today! I love Jesus's opening response about divorce:

> Matthew 19:4 *Haven't you read the Scriptures? Jesus replied. They record that from the beginning 'God made them male and female.*

Jesus knows these highly religious Pharisees have read and, in some cases, memorized the entire Scriptures. By implication, He is suggesting they are ignoring the truth they have been given by God. This is one of His primary complaints with these religious leaders. Today we have the same problem plus people are not reading Scripture at all.

> Matthew 19:6 *Wherefore they are no more twain, but one flesh. What therefore God hath joined together, let not man put asunder.*

In Scripture *"before the New Testament was written"* and in (Genesis 1:24) we see the first marriage between two physical people, Adam and Eve, and further in the same book of Genesis we examine the third couple recorded on Scripture, where this specific story highlights how God brings people together and affirms marriage.

> Genesis 24:67 *And Isaac brought her into his mother Sarah's tent and took Rebekah, and she became his wife; and he loved her: . . .*

Isaac and Rebeca, are a clear example of what marriage really is, they simply entered into a tent and then they were married. The Marriage contract, or better yet the mystery of marriage is a God ordained institution, a mystery until it is revealed, and not any Religious, traditional or government ordained institution. When Isaac and Rebecca got married executed the marriage contract, automatically and naturally with this action of faith they made a sincere commitment to each other and before God. Notice there is no mention of Rebecca's father giving permission, a diamond wedding ring, no mention of human priest conducting any religious ceremony no witnesses present or any so called marriage protocol of tradition such as a dinner feast after, nothing! Therefore official marriage based on scripture is this: Consensual sexual intercourse between two people that decided sincerely by faith to be together is the contract before God.

All of our human traditions, and man made protocols such as the church ritual and wedding feast-reception are exactly as it sounds, they are the introduction to the marriage contract and nothing more, plus they cost too much money, the average cost of a wedding today is around thirty thousand Euros (30.000€), not to mention the house or apartment and the list goes on, as we analyze and break it down to the last detail, money that a lot of people do not have. It is wrong to place in our hearts the tradition and mans law in priority and above Gods law. On the other hand Gods word is clear and simple, and His procedures are free accessible to all, further more it is clear from His word that marriage (unity) as also divorce (separation) occurs in the heart of man, (before the paperwork) and we need to have the same interpretation that God has, or we are doing nothing, rather we are just confidently false assuming of what God really means, falling into the trap of worshiping God in our own assumptions, our own image and that is idolatry.

> *Mark 7:20–23 20 He went on: What comes out of a person is what defiles them. 21 For it is from within, out of a person's heart, that evil thoughts come sexual immorality, theft, murder, 22 adultery, greed, malice, deceit, lewdness, envy, slander, arrogance and folly. 23 All these evils come from inside and defile a person.*

Therefore we need to monitor our hearts and act responsible and slow down and clear up inside our hearts the motivation for our decisions, before taking sudden harsh actions that follow, always aligning with God, not mans opinion. Remember something that looks good can become a bad thing if it keeps us from the very best that God has to offer.

Marriage is a God-ordained institution, a mystery

However it is common sense that the couples have a steady income to support each other, to cover their needs and expenses that they have, and later support their children.

> Genesis 2:24 *That is why a man leaves his father and mother and is united to his wife, and they become one flesh.*

But again, what if the mother and father are already dead and the couple in love does not have the means to live under one roof? Should they live in shame do to ignorance? Pleasing man by sticking to tradition? While the fire of desire consumes them? "*NO!*" Besides having money should not ever be the first criteria, in any decision, rather permission from God should always be our first criteria and His peace in our daily decisions.

In our case *my beloved lady* and I were already both independent responsible middle aged adults, and in love, but we did however lack finance and infrastructure for a traditional-government registered marriage. Also *my beloved lady* did not want to place the burden of the traditional responsibilities of a husband on my shoulders as yet, therefore because she loves me, and really cares for me, was exercising gracefulness and patience in waiting upon God to help us financially, in His perfect timing to become stable in our work, and ready to make further plans, and undertake the financial responsibilities that come with living together, with out any unnecessary migraine headaches.

> Galatians 1:10 *Am I now trying to win the approval of human beings, or of God? Or am I trying to please people? If I were still trying to please people, I would not be a servant of Christ.*

What we learn is tested in how we live the truth, not by what we know as truth.

Chapter 3

God's Providence

ON JUNE 07, 2023 God's *providence*, started a chain of events by honoring us with a gift like no other ever before, lavishing us with what only could God could do to support our unity as a symbol of His acceptance and blessing. The Master Creator set in motion a set of events that favored both *my beloved lady* and I that were inevitable, after much prayer with supplication God permitted our unity by setting up the perfect environment which was Prague in the Czech Republic in the perfect timing with all the necessary funding for us to meet up and to fulfill our marriage contract, according to *His will gave life and power* and not mans tradition.

Just as my plane landed on June/10/2023 I took a taxi and headed towards the hotel in the old city, and on my arrival as I entered the hotel lobby I saw her first, she was waiting for me at the lobby living room area, and my heart was pounding like a drum in my chest, fast and hot in anticipation of her looking my way, all of a sudden as I approached the reception she saw me and we looked at each other, and suddenly a massive flood of adrenaline that shot through me like a drug and made me feel deeply alive.

Our first physical encounter was very comfortable and we did not feel awkward meaning socially uncomfortable; unsure and constrained in any manner, and we do have Jesus to thank for that because he set up the circumstances in a slow delicate manner by diminishing the first impression and observer target, so all of that was solved when we were talking, arguing, debating, making up over the internet so we really have covered two years of video calls which was a great way to keep our relationship strong. There was a time we disagreed on minor things as a couple and she did not want to talk to me, but I made silly efforts to win her back and she was so amused with my silliness that she took me back, I wasn't afraid to lose her because I already had the reassurance that we were meant to be by Jesus, so I felt secure and confident that He will make a way, even when things seemed to be impossible.

This type of communication allowed both of us for more face-to-face time and builded trust and confidence. Our video calls also helped us to build a better relationship and allowed us for open and honest communication between us, and it also provided intimacy and reduced idealization. So because of this long term communication, it took no time at all on our first physical glance, to realize we were ready and both wanted each other.

Therefore dearly beloved friends, relatives and brethren, *my beloved lady* and I were gathered together in agreement with each other and by His will, on Sunday June/11/2023 1:15 p.m. at Hotel Marriott in Prague in the Czech Republic, where we were by faith officially married before God, and we loved each-other. The contract automatically was signed and sealed, because of (1 Peter 2:9), endorsed and executed based on (Genesis 1:24), thus the mystery was substituted with knowledge and we immediately *knew* at the moment we connected and intimate with each other that we were meant and destined for each-other, everything felt so harmoniously right, we were happy and filled with peace and joy, indescribable with just simple words, . . . *just perfect!*

Well surely love was in the air and we both felt it, and there is nothing like true (AGAPI) unconditional sacrificial love, love stands out, its a unique feeling that two people connected can only understand and feel for each-other, and it reflects to others around them, it can not be hid. In Greece we have a saying there are three things one can not hide, the cough, money, and love. Well the other two we surely did not have but love we had in abundance and it showed so much so everyone that saw us knew about our love. True love is rare; we can only hope to find it once in a lifetime, and maybe not even then, but by His grace and mercy we found true love in each other.

We then parted for one week and met each other a second time in Amsterdam on Friday 23/06/2023, where the love, the joy, the celebration and excitement continued this time things were even more intimate and our unity was even stronger than before, it was like every time we separated and re-connected we were deeper into each other, and we loved each other. Our unity in love was like a well known classical music masterpiece, that immediately was executed in a natural harmonic, romantic, pleasant and meaningful way, intensely passionate, filling us with peace, joy, happiness and satisfaction. We were one hundred percent compatible with each other, only a glance was needed for communication as we had the most captivating and intriguing relationship filled with respect for each other and we were open about ourselves, we also both simultaneously gave glory to God for uniting us together, at His perfect timing.

I was in love with her beauty and her passionate heart that poured unconditional love to me, I loved the way she dressed so elegant and wore expensive clothing, and the way she acted when she was in public was also amazing, she was careful with her words, polite a lady modeled civility demonstrating respect, restraint, and personal responsibility in her appearance, behavior, and communication, honorable, values and respect for others, she was a lady well-mannered that knew what was appropriate. I was also very much amused with her sense of humor, which not many could understand (she said) but I did, and I was just as amused with her weakness to be disorganized with her things, she was fragile, mysterious and all woman, and I totally loved caring and chasing after her, placing her things in one place so she could find them easily, and surprisingly because of who she was, automatically became my motivation for a different type of growth, and a higher goal achievement, she made me feel like there were no boundaries and

I wanted to conquer the world for her, I was burning for desire from head to toe.

My beloved lady fell in love with my heart, mind, and loyalty to her, in her difficult moments I was a pillar of steady love she could always lean on, this was something she valued and appreciated in me. She also was in love by the equal way I treated her giving her the respect she deserves, respect that was deprived as a woman from her religious circles. She even asked me once *"why are you so nice to me?"* As I looked straight in to her eyes I honestly and simply replied *"because I love you"* she then smiled perceiving my seriousness and never asked me that question again, as my answer was more than satisfying in her heart and soul.

My beloved lady though not bathed into Scripture as I was, confessed to me this; *"I feel already your wife, and I want to commit and be loyal to you,"* this was her heart and soul speaking out of love for me, I for one also loved her, and of course I knew based on Scripture that I was already her husband, as of 11/06/2023 which was an honor and delight, I just could not share the truth with her as just yet, I felt it was not the right time. I even remember her telling me when we chatted on-line how she hated cooking, well after our intimate get together, she was so emotionally charged in a positive way that she confessed to me that *she had the urge to cook for me*, she said, well how about that!

Later we confessed to each other the same feelings entirely, we felt that we were to each other the last train, the final destination, and we were committed in working to progress towards spending the rest of our lives living and loving each other. We were on the same radio channel transmitting love to each other, aligned with perfect communication with such a harmonious, comfortable unity between us, something like a spiritual and physical agreement, it was just so romantic, and we both wanted this moment to last for ever, and all this to me, was clearly confirmation from God.

Unfortunately time fly's and we are the pilots, on Monday 26/06/2023 we again parted for our current destinations, hoping to quickly meet up and live under one roof, so just as I got back I worked hard trying to make the needful preparations for both our permanent residence in Belgrade Serbia, as we both had agreed upon.

Returning home was not all that bad to be honest, though I would of loved things to go according to a plan I set out, I long for the day when I can say: "*I just love when a good plan comes together.*" Anyway every time I returned to Belgrade at the airport was waiting for me my Business partner and his wife, my beloved brethren in Christ, they saw me first and when I looked around I then saw them, every time I looked at them waiting for me they were with anticipation and joy, they were so cute together, they were side by side and had the same smile with a slight tilt with their head leaning in the same direction like two parrots in love, they were so happy to see me and that really made my day, after we would go to my place and I tell them how I had the time of my life, and how much in love I was with *my beloved lady* and that she is the one for me according to God's divine plan, and so the joy and laughter was shared, as we celebrated every time my return.

After a couple of days rest I had a coffee meeting with a beloved friend and brother from our congregation that really has helped me a lot and always was eager to show practically his love to me, which by the way was one of our congregational leaders.

I immediately said to him that he does not need to worry about me, (because he was always trying to help me find a lady for me to marry, out of concern) so I announced to him that God has taken good care of me and I am officially married by His Grace and mercy.

He was amazed I did not invite him to the wedding and asked some very interesting questions:

1. When were you married?
   June 11, 2023

2. Where were you married?
   Marriott Hotel Prague Czech Republic

3. In what Church were you married at?
   No church, at the Hotel

4. Who was the priest that conducted the wedding ceremony?
   I was! I have the same access to Jesus the eternal priest as everyone else and as king and priest I fulfill Gods requirements.

5. Where is the ceremony, and the rings?
   Sorry I do not have any money for diamond ring and dinner tables, you just have to wait for me on that.

6. What about witnesses?
   The Holy Trinity was invited and was present, the word of God fulfilled testify's our official contract before God, and we were there to practically fulfill the marriage contract before God, so their were five (5) witnesses.

My beloved friend and brother was amazed by my answers and with evidence from scripture, and stated the obvious:

"*I see you have grown in the Lord*".

Unfortunately in his traditional and semi legalistic heart he could not digest what had happened and was searching for a solution to his theory of how marriage aught to be conducted.

So he asked another logical question:

7. Why are you then not living together and are far from each other?
   Because we are gathering money to be together, we do not want financial problems and causing each other migraine issues.

My beloved friend and brother after speaking to *my beloved Lady* and congratulating her and me blessed us. After closing the call even offered to pay for my registry once the time comes and she arrives in Belgrade, HE STILL DIDN'T GET IT! Because tradition is reluctant to change, never the less we finished our coffee and parted joyfully and with hugs.

I do hope the readers of this book are made aware of the problem lack of knowledge of the word of God produces and not only, the biggest problem is that we think we already know, and because we think we know we ignore the little details in scripture that provide the solution.

Of course to my beloved friend and brothers defense, there is another version, because he loves and cares for me, I guess he was eager to celebrate this joyful event with me and even provide a gift for us the couple, but my simplicity and practicality did not permit these things to take effect, I guess that is why we honor the traditional way of the marriage, where there is the ceremony the diner feast and then the bedroom because we can spread and share the joy with our loved ones. Plus all the legal issues are taken care of immediately.

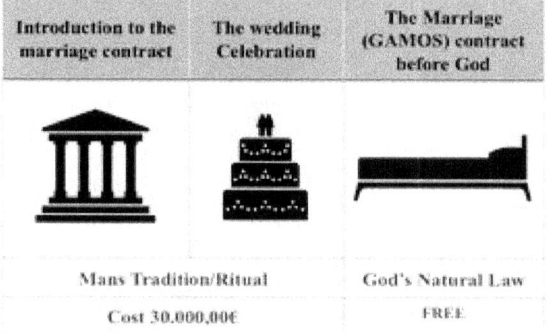

However in our case we had not this opportunity, though we would love to be able to offer the happiness and joy and celebration that everybody was expecting. On the other hand we are hopping in the near future, God willing, to do all the traditional formalities when we legally register ourselves, based on mans traditional law.

Thus why I had to write this here book, not only to gather the right information from scripture, with living proof to teach people that really want to learn, "*Rightly dividing the word of truth.*" But it also saves me time and breath from explaining myself to every Dick, Jane and John that do not read their Bibles, or partly read their Bibles, and even to those that study the Bible, but in different specific subjects.

God's Providence

Preachers and teachers teach that sexual intercourse between a man and a woman is ordained by God within the marriage, and *yes it is true*, however they forgot to tell us that consensual sexual intercourse based on scripture IS THE MARRIAGE! – GAMOS.

What God can not do does not exist

Chapter 4

Law VS Grace

UNDER THE OLD TESTAMENT (Deuteronomy 7:3-4) the Lord gives strict prohibitions against intermarriage, and favors believing marriages (Proverbs 31:30), this way the people of God remained in the faith and a pure bloodline for Jesus to be born. Now that Jesus is born, died, buried, resurrected and alive today, under the New Covenant of grace we are free to choose (1 Corinthians 7:9-15) also notice the verse is direction for a woman not the man and it is given so for the woman's protection, for the women back then had no rights and were considered property, initially of the father before marriage, and after marriage property of the husband.

Now those who just read the surface of the word might say *"in the New Testament God says not to be unequally yoked with unbelievers"*, (2 Corinthians 6:14), *"yes He did"*, and that it is linked to (Deuteronomy 22:9). This verse unfortunately has become a cliche for religious people, mainly (traditionalists, legalists) however the above verse it is specifically not about marriage, or existing marriages. This verse offers a more general principle that the church should keep itself disentangled from fellowship or partnership with pagans, which prohibited yoking together two different animals, it speaks of joining two things that should not be joined. In reality, it will end up being a *"fellowship"* or *"partnership"* in something but it will not be a partnership in the gospel, and therefore it will tend to entangle the believer, in something that might not be kosher. It really applies to any environment where we let the world influence our thinking. When we are being conformed to this world and are not being transformed by the renewing of our mind (Romans 12:2), we join together with unbelievers in an ungodly way. Paul is not suggesting that Christians never associate with unbelievers, the principle is that we are to be in the world, but not of the world, like a ship should be in the water, but water shouldn't be in the ship. If the world is influencing us, it is clear we are unequally yoked together with unbelievers, and the most important factor, as we approach the ideas and values of the world we are distancing ourselves from God and approaching closer to the enemy and by doing so we automatically declare war on God (Romans 8:6), so we need to be very careful, for our spiritual pleasure to be greater then our physical pleasure, not to disregard scripture, and not caring more of what the world is thinking about us rather than our spiritual family, however if we do catch ourselves slipping God does offer us the solution on how to recover.

> James 4:7 *Submit yourselves therefore to God. Resist the devil, and he will flee from you.*

As a yoke for marriage, yes it is practical for a common direction in faith for two people, and for both to also equally share the same burdens in life, but this is not a law.

Jesus died for all, God's grace is undeserved favor, grace cannot be earned; it is something that is freely given, grace is a part of God's character it is the bridge He built in our relationship with Him, therefore our influence should be rock solid in the Lord, not in our own comfort zone. If the believers are not bathed into scripture and one with God, and in todays busy society when in a household God takes slowly the back seat and prayer becomes the spare tire rather than the steering wheel, then there are no guarantees, of any long term successful marriage.

My beloved lady is a God fearing woman, sincere, and honest, its just that her belief system is different, and okay a bit spoiled, as she is from a wealthy family, with maids serving her needs, and drivers taking her everywhere. I only dreamed of having such service, and despite the difference in status, God permitted the unity of *my beloved lady* and I after securing everything for a whole year initially on an emotional level, because of our past traumas, so at that time there wasn't a shadow of a doubt that we were meant to be together and God was with us, (because I invited Him, I have the same access to Jesus as everyone else, God and I are in excellent relations and communication), and so by faith we loved each other and our bed was undefiled, we felt peace, joy and we were happy, and all was well with us. *My beloved lady* was a hidden treasure a rare jewel with amazing gifts, my heart melted like butter only by the way she looked at me, like I had value and worth, and that made me feel good inside, and so I was ready to give her everything, just to make her happy, the mystery was revealed and we knew each other. Please note that, mystery based on ancient Greek meaning is not something that is unknown, rather it is something that can only be known by revelation, and in this case by "*knowing each other*".

Just as our short summer vacation time in Europe ended we finally went back to where God had initially placed us, *my beloved lady* returned to Jakarta Indonesia and I returned to Belgrade Serbia. We were both in love so we continued to communicate via internet again and longing to be together on a permanent basis, dreaming to live in our own house. After a couple of months of prayer supplication and eagerly waiting for an opportunity to be together again, God finally opens a door for our company bringing in new business opportunities that financed our business activities.

> Proverbs 10:22 *The blessing of the LORD brings wealth, without painful toil for it.*

To be very honest I was starting to fall into depression as we drew closer to the holiday season, I was thinking that money was tight and clients will start to make excuses not to buy or pay their obligations and we would probably be alone and far from our families again, basically we looked at all holiday seasons as hell! But all caring and all loving God had made preparations to bless us and give us happiness and fill us with His Joy, simultaneously receiving all the glory for He only could do what was going to follow.

On November 23/2023 God's providence knitted together the fulfillment of yet another dream by providing all the funding needed for *my beloved lady* and I to schedule a Christmas and new year vacation together for thirteen days 22/12/23–03/01/24 in Lombok Indonesia, so we may continue to be together and enjoy life after our marriage contract had successfully been fulfilled, after all God united us now God keeps and sustains us, moving us slowly to the next level of intimacy and commitment. The Joy, the happiness that I felt was indescribable.

Blessed is the one that God's will is aligned with ones heart desire!

I issued my airline ticket in the beginning of December reserving a good deal on the flight ticket and hotel, *my beloved lady* on the other hand issued her ticket around the seventeen of December much later and was requesting from the same local airline company seats next to each other, however the ticket agency told her that this was impossible and she was a bit upset that we would not be sitting next to each other on the same plane, so I calmly and politely said to her *"at least we will go and land together"*. Again on our boarding day from Jakarta airport *my beloved lady* attempted on check in to get seats next to each other, sadly the check in clerk said we will not be sitting next to each other but across from eachother. However the Master Knitter and Organizer of the universe had other plans, little did anyone know that the airline switched planes that day to a new and bigger model, and so in the end we got seats next to each other and we remained in awe with what God had programmed for us, as we were holding each others hand we both gave glory to God all the way to our final destination where we were picked up by the hotel taxi service.

As I entered the reception of the hotel resort there was a warm welcome and as I greeted everyone they were all smiling and the atmosphere was pleasant and joyous. The receptionist on duty testified much later after we got to be friends that when the reception team first met me after I greeted them they saw I was a humble man, and every time I passed by the reception their was a sparkle of joy and peace that came along with me and spread not only at the reception but "my beloved lady" testified that everyone that had contact with us, the staff reception-restaurant, cleaners all liked me, and some wanted to relate to me in some formal way, there was this waiter also that greeted me with a good morning in Greek Καλημέρα that is pronounced (Kalimera). Now this is the work of the Holy Spirit working inside me all theses years and was transforming my character closer to the likeness of Jesus as matter of fact the Holy Spirit in me was doing all the work, transmitting through me love, peace and joy, so much so everyone that came across *my beloved lady* and I loved us, and she was amazed by peoples warm reaction towards us.

There was this other waiter that noticed how much in love we were and offered us a hotel package deal to have a romantic dinner overlooking the sea with our choice of drinks, wine or champagne with a live classical orchestra and candle light, the whole package of a romantic dinner, but unfortunately the price was a bit high and we both agreed it wasn't worth it.

I was amazed to what God had slowly transformed me into, a couple of years back *"humble"* was not the word that would describe me, but now on account of His work in me it was so. God loves me so much that He would not leave me as I was, and slowly through every storm transformed me and continues transforming me into His likeness, His character because He is gentle and humble in heart, that I may abide with Him, to Him be the glory honor and praise forever.

My beloved lady and I were in love and on fire, our third encounter was even stronger than the previous two, the first was the execution of the contractual marriage the second a short holiday vacation, with a little more intimacy, and this one was more like a proper honeymoon. We freely expressed our love every day three times a day like there is no tomorrow, tirelessly for an hour and a half, we were inseparable and we just could not get enough of each other, well what can one expect after seven years of desert loneliness, simultaneously our love was therapeutic from our past marriage traumas that we both had. We trusted each other on a whole different level and understood each others needs and just like that we were free to explore by serving one another in a way that satisfied our body soul and mind, we connected like two lego pieces made by God for one another in amazing perfect harmony. We were so happy and exited, I loved her sense of humor, even when expressing herself freely with words such as "*alleluia thank you Jesus*" and "*this is Sparta*". In general *my beloved lady* made me feel like a man especially when complimenting me for my performance or endurance as a ten years younger than my age, I for one gave praise to God for everything, because our patience all these years was finally rewarded. We were both living in paradise for thirteen days and in complete agreement with each other, giving and receiving nothing more than (AGAPI) unconditional, sacrificial, pure love, that reflected on the whole resort, everybody knew about us! We even prayed together before each meal we had by giving thanks in the name of Jesus, that we both said amen to. There are three things you can not hide we say in Greece, the cough, money, and love, and love we certainly did have plenty of that, so much so it reflected on our daily lives. Okay I am boasting a bit, but for good reason, you see I had friends that did not have any trust in God at all, (obviously, how can anyone trust someone they do not know) they actually believed that one must sleep with a woman to know whether or not they were meant to be, which really was just another excuse for having sexual intercourse. On the other hand I trusted all knowing God to pick a wife for me, His timing also, and by faith I accepted His choice of spouse even when storms appeared and He chose perfectly for me, whereas now I am happy, content and satisfied, so much so, that I have to confess that Gods reality is better than or tops up, all my deepest most intimate fantasies, (Ephesians 3:20).

My beloved lady and I had such perfect communication between us that she was also open to Scripture accepting the word of God, sharing my simple explanation and providing proof from (Genesis 24:67) that on 11/06/2023 under God we were already officially married, and yes I did finally share that vital bit of information, Knowing the truth is important and liberating but wisdom is knowing when and how to express the knowledge that one has, avoiding unnecessary migraines and of course as a lady she desired a ring, which I gladly provided one for her.

Another thing I loved about her was she knew how to dress, her choice of clothing was simple elegant, she looked good in everything she wore because of her thin and beautiful figure, its funny as a single man that was used to getting dressed and exiting the premises now I found myself waiting a half an hour for *my beloved lady* to prepare herself, so this was kind of a new thing for me, perceiving my thoughts she politely said to me: "*if you wait for me a while you will surely enjoy the results.*" You know what? She was absolutely right, when preparing for dinner she was breathtaking and I definitely enjoyed the results so much so I gladly waited for her every day with out even caring about the time.

Now because of *my beloved lady's* family business and various religious commitments we agreed that a government marriage and ceremony would take some time, and we were both okay and at peace with this arrangement, we just simply wanted to be together, we did not care about any paperwork, by yielding and satisfying mans religious, and traditional points of view.

Things were going so perfect that on December 31, 2023 we were all enjoying New Years dinner together with her family (mom her two sisters plus *My beloved lady* and of course me), the food and drinks were excellent, I had all the sea food I could get my hands on from the buffet such things as lobster, clams, shrimps, then when the D.J. started the program and the music started we all (except mom) danced to the music and just had loads of fun. Then when the raffle started we sat down at our table taking a short break while looking at our raffle tickets numbers if we won anything, but as time went by everyone else gave up and stopped looking at their raffle ticket numbers and did not expect to win anything, then all of a sudden they announced one of my ticket numbers and the table lit up in excitement, as I had excitedly shouted "*I WON!!!*" I had won an extra night stay at the hotel resort, everyone was amazed, they could not believe that our table won something, and after being congratulated by everyone, even the waiters at the table, I went to claim my prize. The next morning after breakfast I went to see how I could claim on my prize, and so because of my flight schedule the hotel management was kind enough to change it to an open credit line of one hundred Euros.

WELL GUESS WHAT!?!

For two days *my beloved lady* and I and especially in the evenings sat romantically at a table overlooking the sea admiring the sunset with food and drinks for free. God had arranged to treat us a romantic dinner for two! I have no words to describe my feeling of gratitude towards God!

On January 03 2024 we both returned to where God had stated us, *my beloved lady* in Jakarta Indonesia and I returned to Belgrade Serbia, we spent a couple of hours in the Jakarta airport she kept me company and at first we were sad for parting with each other but as time came to part the joy of what God had done for us prevailed thinking that we had the time of our lives. For me it was true, this was the best vacation in my entire life up to now, so we parted at the airport with peace and anticipation with the hope that soon enough money will roll in and we will be together, so when I was alone I asked God, "*now what Lord? Since You have proven many times that You care so much for us and our happiness, what is next God?*" I was eager and so exited to see what will God's love and goodness will permit next in our lives, I was certain, and without a reasonable doubt that God was working, knitting together to reveal His next dosage of love.

Let's face it, a lot of marriages fail due to unbearable financial problems, that spring up within the marriage causing great deal of discomfort, followed by lack of communication due to stress and anxiety that leads to breakdown and finally to separation. Many years we struggled to make ends meet, we faced financial business problems like everyone else, our church was a help and support but there is so much an organization can do especially when one reaches deep waters with massive waves and storms. However difficult the situation with debts piling up, as faithful stewards of our company we looked to Jesus's eyes and not the storms, we remained positive ignoring as leaders negativity and slander, united in prayer and intercession for our business and families. We worked hard, focused on our goal with patience sacrificing for what we believed and wanted, rather our dreams becoming the sacrifice, so we were consistent, disciplining ourselves and motivating each other to press on forward with confidence in God's promises to us, for this was not just one battle but a war, that kept us up on our toes for years, but we trusted God giving Him the steering wheel to metaphorically; captain our boat, that reached uncharted deep waters to lead us to a safe and peaceful harbor. The fact is that God only gives and when He does not give, we do not have, and I deeply longed to be a stable husband for "my beloved lady", a provider for my family once again. So I stand on God's faithfulness to me, rather than my faithfulness to Him.

Law VS Grace

Chapter 5

Not called to do, but to trust Him

THERE ARE THOSE WHO work for God, and those who work with God, in relationship and partnership with Him and the difference is the result, in us and around us (Matthew 7:21–23).

> Zechariah 4:6 ... *Not by might, nor by power, but by my spirit, saith the Lord of hosts.*

Nothing needs to be added to Scripture; we are thoroughly equipped for serving God through God's Word. When Jesus was teaching His disciples how to pray Jesus taught after praising and giving glory to the Father.

> Matthew 6:10 *Your kingdom come, your will be done, on earth as it is in heaven.*

Why? Because if we really trust God and we are confident that He loves us then we already know that His will is to our benefit, His will is the solution to our problem because He is the ancient of days and He knows how things work better than us, and His will triumphs over all situations, and for more good news His will is something that He can teach us to do (Psalm 143:10), so we can rely on His guidance and instruction always, and can rest assure we will always triumph in the long run. God's will, by which He works out all things according to His purpose, is a wonderful comfort to believers, and nothing in our life is outside of God's purpose or beyond His control. Now, exactly how the events of our lives are woven into the Father's plan, we cannot tell, but that is okay we trust Him, we know He loves us (John 3:16).

They say money can not buy happiness, now please note; joy comes from God and it is based on our relationship with God, happiness is based on happenings, it's goal oriented and we do not find it we make it, so when certain people say that money can not buy happiness well they lie to us, maybe they do not know that money can actually buy happiness, you see as example money buys me coffee and coffee makes me happy, its that simple!

All those that are in business are taught by the more experienced entrepreneurs that there are three things we must keep a secret, our financial situation, (how much we earn) our love life, (is nobody's business) and our next move, (avoid conflict and judgmental negative behavior) and this because of peoples jealousy, the truth is not everyone rejoices when we are happy. However WE ARE NOT SAVED TO BE SILENT (Romans 1:16) to watch people suffer and close up inside because they are misinformed and certain subjects are neglected to be taught, maybe people are not interested in depth to talk about matters in (Marriage and money), maybe people are too comfortable leaving things traditionally where they are at, or worse people's false impression that they already know, maybe those who do actually know do not want the headache of criticism from public opinion, what ever the case may be, I am so past shallow doctrine (fast food or milk for babies) being served in congregations all over the world. I guess I can write a whole book accusing the confident Pharisee, the good moralist, the experimentalist trusting his feelings, the opinionist with their perfect doctrine, but I say *"love don't judge."* I choose to labor with boldness, searching scriptures and with the help of The Holy Spirit serving the truth, like the Apostles before me writing and preaching the Gospel, that covers in detail (if one looks deep enough), all subjects of life that provides freedom from the law and mans traditions, rather their focus was to guide people to a direct relationship with Jesus and only Jesus as the only high priest, and not to themselves. Therefore I will follow the same example that Scripture teaches us practically, that if you and I have grown in some area beyond milk, and are in meat, we should share and teach that truth (humbly, patient) to those less mature, rather than merely seeking more meat for ourselves. *God commanded us to make disciples not converts.*

Beloved try to understand spiritual meat does not force a believer to respond to a law; it prompts beyond this, to respond to a relationship with the Spirit (Galatians 5:18). Milk and meat, as in any healthy diet, should be balanced and served properly in small portions. The milk drinker honors a set of rules. The meat eater desires to honor God and people. A person who takes only milk desires to push the limits. Meat eaters desire to steer clear of limits. Milk is law. Meat is love. Milk is the baby's desire to do what he's told. Meat is the believer's passion to obey God only because he is deeply in love with Him. Milk drinkers find comfort in the crowd and are effected by other believers. Meat eaters look into Jesus's eyes and follow Him. A mature follower of Christ (one who can eat spiritual meat), has trained himself to distinguish good from evil (Hebrews 5:14), because he spends regular time in God's presence, in God's word and in prayer.

Also the meat, the solid food that Jesus, Paul and Peter are referring to is not just teaching, but rather doing the works of Jesus! Doing the works of Jesus or working to finish what Jesus has revealed to us to do, is next level apprenticeship in the kingdom, where the Holy Spirit teaches us how to go deeper in Him. Some things in the kingdom that can only be learned through doing, and by doing we achieve experienced first hand knowledge, and that will also lead in deeper knowledge of certain parts of scripture that we simply read and passed on by. In other words we are transformed into the fresh new Gospel, the continuing of the book of Acts, chapter twenty nine (29).

We grow because of our understanding of His righteousness.

Our understanding of His version of righteousness not ours, brings growth. God's love grace and mercy is greater than other peoples opinion about us, even of our own selves.

I would like to challenge believers all over the world to step beyond a list of rules and seek a loving relationship direct with God, because that is the essence of a meaty doctrine, thus why I want to share my personal testimony in these matters. *"If you are ever tempted to look for outside approval, realize that you have compromised your integrity",* inside you is more power than you will ever know, the question is whether you are using it or not. No more people telling you what to do and being mislead, deceived and psychologically destroyed, feeling guilt and remorse because one desires a relationship, and to feel the warmth of a companion, just because the protocol of tradition does not permit or worse judge those who do not follow the protocol, on account of their lack of proper knowledge and teaching in depth. Therefore, I need the truth about the grace of the Gospel concerning this very little mentioned and sensitive subject and the example of my experience about the contract of Marriage before God, to get out into public knowledge, to reveal with the help of my short practical testimony that, we should not mix the broom with the mop, what I mean is this; Tradition is not God's law, and when we make man made tradition more important than God's word, then we insult Him.

The marriage contract is an automatic unity system (there is no test drive) as is child birth blessed and ordained by God it is His automated system, God the almighty, Omnipotent responds to faith, He responds to belief, and a simple practical supplement is as follows:

1. If the God fearing couple (Man & Woman) agree to be together, and they want to wait after the traditional protocol of a religious/government ceremony to fulfill the marriage contract between them and God, this is okay and they are not sining, if they are strong and can wait, good for them, without pride judging others for not following the protocol. Jesus was invited and went to such ceremonies like the recorded wedding in Cana (John 2:11).

2. If the God fearing couple (Man & Woman) do not want to wait and both desire the marriage contract to be fulfilled,

because of their financial status that does not permit anytime soon for a traditional Religious and government wedding ceremony and desire each other, they are not sining if they conduct the marriage contract as (Genesis 24:67) before God, and merciful loving caring God explains why we are not sinning.

> 1 Corinthians 7:9b . . . *for it is better to marry than to burn.*

This because the religious traditional ceremony-ritual followed by celebration is not the marriage contract that God has ordained, and God is everywhere (Jeremiah 23:23–24).

I too respect the value of the practicality of tradition, and legal registry with the Government, which by the way does not enforce on a couple WHEN they should register. I am just explaining the true meaning with examples and commentary of the Greek word for marriage (Gamos) that is also in our Bible, of God's intended meaning. Therefore people stop worrying because if God is with us then no one can be against us, (Colossians 2:16–17), let not any man judge, or apply a set of legal rules upon us, no man is authorized by God to judge, and control another in any way, therefore we can now all relax, and let God continue to rule the universe.

3. When a man and a woman agree and come together for pleasure only, God still honors the marriage contract no matter what the motivation (1 Corinthians 6:16), even the physical law on pregnancy when the joined couple is not careful, however when they separate also willingly, they are committing divorce (ripping apart) which also begins in the heart, and that is sin.

> Matthew 19:6 *What therefore God hath joined together, let not man put asunder.*

God puts something together, man has no business changing it or breaking it apart, because God hates divorce (Malachi 2:16), however loving God is compassionate merciful and forgiving, and on account of the cross, just like any other sin it is forgivable just the same BUT… the after effect, the consequences of the pain (the ripping apart), will follow.

My mother's advice to me a long time ago was: *"your signature and your penis you must be careful where you put it."* Excellent advice, however I need to work still on my . . . signature.

Consider the Samaritan woman a well known story in (John 4:16–18). The Samaritan woman slept with five people that Jesus called them husbands! Number six did not get as far.

> John 4:18 *"The fact is, you have had five husbands, and the man you now have is not your husband."*

She was trying to fill her need to feel loved and acceptance, however we see that there is a space that only God can fill in our heart and soul, thus her reaction later in the story, she wasn't physically thirsty but spiritually thirsty for God, the only one filling her emptiness. It was brought to her attention with Jesus's way of teaching, patiently, with love helping her see clearly so she can make freely the right decision concerning her need and allowing her to take immediate positive action.

The *"marriage protocol"* that is the ceremony and legal registry that has become necessary for the reason being we as people are impatient, stiff-necked hard hearted, and make bad choices when thinking with the desire of our flesh rather than using God's peace His Spirit of direction. We do not consult anyone anymore yet alone God that invented the marriage mystery to wait and receive His peace as confirmation. So the Church in association with the state (Man) has invented the *"marriage protocol"* that we know and have today, to organize people better to help people think clearly and commit to each other after the passion has faded so no one gets hurt, especially the children if any. All this is fine but the church and the state have however forgotten to inform the young couple that the government registry and church ritual is as it sounds, its the introduction of the marriage, the official Marriage contract before God is in the bedroom, and that is the official marriage before God, and most people think, because the wedding bed is a natural expectation, that the bedroom scene is simply a natural follow through. We simply have to reverse this misconception in young peoples minds and teach the truth, and not leave the young generation ignorant to blind chance hopping they will think to figure it out on their own. It is wrong to place in our hearts the tradition and mans law in priority and above Gods law.

We have a responsibility to inform people correctly to help sharpen their conscience and their ability to tell right from wrong, praying for ourselves and for others, that we may all be guided in our choices and that we may have love toward one another.

> 1 Timothy 1:5 *The aim of our charge is love that issues from a pure heart and a good conscience and a sincere faith.*

God is love and unlimited, however that does not exclude the fact that He is also the Judge, plus what God can not do, does not exist. He is the God that does not come anywhere uninvited and when invited, and out of love and concern He turns water into the best tasting wine ever, God really cares about us. Notice what Jesus did as a guest to the wedding of Cana, the capacity of the water was (120 and 180 gallons, or 681,37 liters), that was turned into wine, let's think about this, there's not a wedding party on earth that can drink that much wine. Why that much? Jesus gave a luxurious gift to this couple, if they wanted they could easily sell it and live off the proceeds for a long time, and the quality was very good, one could say heavenly. It was just a way to bring joy to be able to enjoy this blessing for weeks and months.

There is only one God, and He loves us all the same, despite our different denominations, philosophies and theories, further more (Agape) love does not dominate it cultivates sound doctrine, God does not hate or judge us, God respects and loves us with a unique kind of unconditional love, He wants to help us break free to change our thinking because we are His weakness, Jesus is the same yesterday, today and forever, and He is the only priest we need. Therefore we must not give control over our lives to any man, (*we all have the same access to Jesus*) above all we should not place mans tradition in a priority and higher that God's Holy Word, or we are insulting God. Therefore we must not just read His word on the surface, and cling to our own understanding, but take seriously time to study God's word in depth. We must take time searching scripture, finding key word meaning, analyze history, and the Holy Spirit will help open our mind and change our way of thinking, to discover the truth, which by the way is the point of the Greek word repent, pronounced metanoia - (*Μετάνοια*), meaning to change ones type of thinking, not not just saying we are sorry, but works of faith must follow, not neglecting to pray and be in constant communication with our creator through Jesus our mediator, because personal communication with God (intimacy) is the key to a successful life.

Chapter 6

Love by chance, stay by choice

AGAPI LOVE IS NOT merely a decision and a choice, its much more, its a desire its an affection, that has to do with the one giving it not the one receiving it. Love is greater than faith and hope because love is eternal, while faith and hope are temporal (1 Corinthians 13:8–13). Therefore we fell in love by chance, and we chose to stay in love by choice.

Relationships last not because they were destined to last, but because two people made a choice to keep it, fight for it and work for it. "*I chose to love you forever, my beloved lady!*"

> Proverbs 18:22 *Whoso findeth a wife findeth a good thing, and obtaineth favour of the Lord.*

One day when we were swimming in the hotel pool *My beloved lady* looked at me with admiration in her eyes and said to me that, she was approached by many wealthy suitors but she turned them all down to be with me, "*you are very expensive*" she said to me, and confided in me the reason was that, not only she deeply loved me, which I felt was the truth, but also because with me she was free to be and express herself, and she was relieved that I accepted and loved her for who she really was. *My beloved lady* was also very appreciative that I came to her after so many hours of flight precisely forty three hours, with stops along the way (transit) and she considered me a hero and a strong man that did not give up in any way on her. I am thinking, *"wow!!!"* To me it was actually nothing, and I gladly for her do the same thing one thousand times over again. *My beloved lady* was so happy that out of love she said: "*I finally found a man that really loves me,*" this statement made me very happy, for it is one thing to give love and another to accept and receive it, my love was clearly understood. As we embraced and kissed each other it began to rain, and everyone left the pool area, we looked around and saw we were all alone, we didn't care about the rain and continued making love in the water, that day we gave new meaning to the phrase water sports. Then the rain stoped, and we exited the pool only to continue the love passion and desire at our bungalow, that's how much in love we were, exploiting every opportunity we had to express our love for one another.

I also had the privilege to meet *my beloved lady's* mother that was a very nice, polite lady and a talented oil painter, she prayed for me and my work to succeed, one day I was invited at her moms house for lunch and we exchanged ideas on oil painting, mom the two sisters and I connected immediately and I loved them and they all loved me back as well, they were all really simple and nice people. We also visited some friends of hers and dined out with them at a traditional restaurant, one close lady friend of *my beloved lady's*, said to her something funny complimenting me: "*where did you find this handsome man?*" We all laughed and joked around, everyone was happy and there was only love in the atmosphere, and no mention of any form or obstacles of religion. Religion has no place in any person's life, God is love not religion. Religion separates people, Gods love unites people. Religion is a tool of the educated to manipulate the uneducated, so people be cautious what you hear.

1. Religion (Self Effort, Works)

- Goal: reach out to God and try to work your way into heaven, adding to Jesus's finished work.

- Means: diligent service & works, with hopes of a reward (heaven)
- Power: good, honest effort through self-determination
- Control: self-motivation and self control

The Results: apathy, failure, chronic guilt, eternal separation from God. Insulting Jesus and false perception that if we do something God will love us more, however God never loved us less.

2. God Salvation Through Faith In Jesus Christ (Personal Relationship, Intimacy).

- Goal: trust fully in Jesus, then live to please Him
- Means: confess sins, repent, yield self to Jesus
- Power: the Holy Spirit does God's work in and through us
- Control: allow the Holy Spirit to control & direct our lives

The Results: love, joy, peace, freedom, victory, power, eternal life in heaven, Jesus is enough.

Man's way to reach God is religion, but God's way to reach man is Jesus

The biggest obstacle for one to learn, is not the willingness to read or to listen, but the false perception one already knows.

The enemy of the Gospel is religion that says if I believe the right things and live right way I will be saved, God should take care of me. We are like a person that thinks Christianity is a set of rules to follow rather than warm, sincere relationship with Christ.

So what is my hope in? My hope is in myself, self salvation not in the truth which is God's mercy and grace. *Salvation is a gift not a transaction!*

> John 14:6 *"I am the way, the truth, and the life. No one may come to the Father except through me."* Paul writes in,

> Ephesians 2:8-9 *For by grace are you saved, through faith; and this not of your own, it is the gift of God. Not of works, lest any man should boast.*

I have been struggling with storms and waves for a long time, so much so that Jesus used this time to change my prideful character to a humble one. The truth is that struggle develops character, the diamond is formed under pressure, the seed grows in darkness, and the olive is crushed for the precious oil, so when there is struggle what one becomes in the process of fulfilling any dream is more important than the dream itself. The person becomes humble, patient, faithful, manifesting a character Jesus develops in a person is extraordinary. As a man rises in the morning and walks and talks with a different spirit, and others notice, people know that person knows about life, he is trusted as one who has experience and embraced life. Without struggle there is no progress, life is not measured by the number of breaths we take, but by the moments that take our breath away. Storms will always come and go, they are part of our life, that is why Jesus takes the time to teach us how to sail through them all, while simultaneously transforming our character into His likeness, and helps us by teaching us to think differently to see things as He the Ancient of days knows how everything and all works.

If life is not a challenge please check your pulse

My beloved lady has certainly taken my breath away, her beauty astonishes me, her regal character intrigues me, her voice is hypnotic and my heart in her presence skips a beat, I long to be with her, my desire is for us to be together from here and after, I do not want to waste any more time apart from her, and just as I long to be with her, I also felt deep in my heart that her presence alone was satisfactory reward for me. A man settles where he finds peace, not beauty not money, not status but peace, the truth is with her I feel peace, *"she makes me feel like I am finally home."* In her presence I can be my genuine self and not hide in any defense mechanism for survival, I feel free to be me, with the reassurance I will be loved and accepted.

All these emotions that sprung up and I naturally felt was the trigger of revelation used by the Holy Spirit to teach and reveal to me that this is what the Lord desires for us to be like, we tend to forget that God is a living God with real feelings and emotions just like us that we were created in His image, transmitting love twenty four-seven patiently waiting and looking for us to notice Him and just love Him for who He really is. Just as this revelation hit me, looking back on the journey to get to this stage today, after noticing His love and sensitivity to my feelings and emotions and desires, I came to realize that His presence is my reward. I long to be in His presence, He is my gold and precious jewel, He is my joy, my peace, He makes me feel like home away from home.

Just as I want *my beloved lady* to be happy, I want to feel God smile and be happy with me, Just as I confess *My beloved lady* to people with boldness, in the same manner I confess Jesus, because I delight in Him. I truly feel that He loves me unconditionally despite the fact that He knows who I really am deep inside, better than I do. I love to hear His voice captivating my heart and mind. Now more than ever I realize that our reward in heaven is Jesus, for He is my peace, joy, my righteousness, He is my life itself and that in abundance, what a wonderful counselor, a loving caring Shepherd, an awesome God He is.

In business it is not what you know but "*Who*" you know, and our character determines whether or not we will stand in that special or important "*Who's*" presence (Genesis 41:1–36), Pharaoh was Joseph's biggest investor, and he spoke as we should with knowledge and *humility*. Pride is like ones bad breath, where everyone else notices it except the one having it, and needs to be dealt with or in Josephs case he could of very well lost his head if it wasn't for God's boot camp to train him to be humble. We are destined to be with Jesus and we go to heaven because we know Him for He is the Door (John 10:9), therefore we have salvation because of who we know, and He is humble, and so should we, or else we can not walk with God.

> Proverbs 22:4 *Humility is the fear of the LORD; its wages are riches and honor and life.*

This verse by the way is the secret to success and riches in life, the key is humility, just look at the richest people in the world they all have one thing in common, and that is humility, whereas because of their humble state, God can actually work with them.

On Thursday 29/02/2024 God set up again a chain of events providing miraculously all our needs via our network. A check is as good as the one issuing it, and God's promise is something everyone with assurance can take to the bank.

> Proverbs 16:3 *Commit thy works unto the Lord, and thy thoughts shall be established.*

Meaning *we need to learn how to think right before we can start to live right.* Successful living begins on earth not passively waiting for it in heaven. God reminded His promise to me given thirty two years ago on 29/02/1992 (Psalm 37:4), date and verse hand written on my old Bible, and so it turns out that eight, four-year terms took my healing-teaching and re-moulding journey of my character in the wilderness, my assignment was my confinement, now finally exited and humbly entered into His rest, my promised land, had begun to reveal itself before me.

On May 19th to 30, 2024 God's *providence*, started a chain of events by honoring us once again, lavishing us with the funding for a vacation time in Bali Indonesia, this time not only to support our unity as a symbol of His acceptance and blessing, but also to reveal and teach us how life would be like by living together under one roof, as this was our deepest desire. Ten days we spent together in Bali Indonesia and again our unity was stronger than before and it was very different than all the other times we were together, even though we followed a steady daily routine, it wasn't monotonous or boring, as each others presence alone filled our spirit heart and soul and the love we shared was this time meaningful with a sense of common purpose.

After waking up early in the morning around 7:30–8:00 am and after a short prayer we made our way to the breakfast lounge for our standard breakfast, and shortly after breakfast we then returned to our room changed to our bathing suits and covered our bodies with tanning oil with the smell of coconut and swam enjoying the coolness of the refreshing water with a dash of foreplay in the hotel pool, before going back to our room where love took over on a more intimate level and because it was with meaning and purpose it lasted no less than one hour, not because we were finished, not so, we were tired, the truth is we could not get enough of each other. When we got hungry we went out to lunch walking on the wider side of the sidewalk trying to avoid along the way merchants that tried to convince us to buy souvenirs from them, people constantly asking if we want to rent a motor bike and or taxi service, while looking and trying to choose the desired place for us to eat, also trying to avoid beggars and people pushing promotional leaflets, while simultaneously monitoring with our ears for any motor scooters trying to dodge traffic on the opposite direction of the road behind us. After lunch we walked back to the hotel taking the beach sidewalk near the sea side only to discover that it was filled with small cantinas selling a seat to monitor the sunset and people offering to give us foot massages. Never the less we focused on each other rather the noise and tried to make the best of our ten minute walk. We finally got back to the hotel where we dozed off next to each other for about two hours before going out near by for coffee and later on for dinner if we were hungry and drinks while following the same path and avoiding the same people. Later in the evening as we returned to our room in one piece, showered and made love making every second together count, the anticipation of being together is a lot more than words can describe, in a way that's so completely tangible. One touch and the intoxication is instant, whatever we want to do is what we do, no hesitations. Just her scent sends me into a heady trance, one that doesn't end until our bodies are still once more, just warm and snuggled in as close as two souls can be.

    We then laid in bed slightly exhausted holding hands watching a movie together even one we have seen before and just enjoyed each others fellowship, and as the movie continued softly playing she doze off first next to me and I sat until the movie was over before turning off the TV and going to sleep, with the eagerness and anticipation to wake up next to *my beloved lady* and feel her warm hug and warm hand touching my face once again, while looking into her eyes as she was transmitting with a simple gaze a wide range of emotions establishing a deep connection, her eyes communicated empathy and understanding making me feel of great value to her.

One might think a ten day routine, in some things yes, but everyday felt totally different, even though we were on vacation and the actions might of been the same more or less but the feelings of intimacy and love we expressed and felt for each other were indeed very different on a daily basis and very fulfilling, as a matter of fact when we were in our room and just simply sitting together, we did not feel like we were in Bali Indonesia, or anywhere for that matter, as long as we were together we felt so complete with each other, so much so that time (we never really looked at our watches) and the place was irrelevant to us, it was a peculiar feeling that we both loved and desired to keep forever, it also inspired into us the saying: *"the journey does not matter as much, as who one takes the journey with."* Together we felt like we were already home (not caring where we are) we simply felt peace, and so much joy as we were happy to be and live together, I guess we realized now more than ever that we were consciously loving each other and ready to commit to each-other and live under one roof, we felt that we were ready to move together with God to the next level, things were so mature that *my beloved lady* for the first time agreed finally with me and asked for us to get a legal government marriage certificate and that either in Greece or Serbia.

Now preparing to go out had its funny challenges too, as *my beloved lady* kept misplacing certain little things leaving them here and there and even though it was a small bungalow looking for a pair of glasses could be a challenge, luckily I remembered where she used them last and double backed and found them for her, and I just loved when she thanked me like I was her hero, I felt so proud that I could save the day. So then after these incidents I proposed to buy a small house with minimalistic design to live in so I don't spend too much time looking for things, and she laughed and agreed with me.

Two days during the week we had various business activities to attend to together, we were invited for lunch and dinner the next day by a business colleague of *My beloved lady's* as she is a well known bank analyst with a good reputation and people often called her for advice.

After the first event *my beloved lady* booked us for a SPA at the hotel, me for a full body massage and a pedicure for herself, this was funny and intriguing at the same time, because I loved the way she pampered me, especially when examining in choosing the right place (it took her three days to decide) and the lady that will place her hands on me for the full body massage.

One afternoon we were invited by *my beloved lady's* sister and husband which was from Germany and living in Bali years now, to go out to eat at a special and famous restaurant that even Mick Jagger ate there, and so after a great time of fellowship they drove us back to the hotel. Traffic was horrible but I noticed along the way awesome souvenir shops and wood handcrafted furniture shops, amazing works of art. I also noticed these brand new red color public busses, fully air-conditioned, that fit around twenty people with a yellow bar in front of them, so I asked *my beloved lady's* brother in law what the bars were and he replied they are for placing bicycles on them. I was amazed by this feature that the busses had, then I was asked to notice that the busses were empty inside, when I asked why, I was told that nobody rides them because the local citizens can not get to the buss stop to take the bus, that was funny, because to get to the bus stop one had to take a motorcycle or car and there was no parking to leave the vehicle, and if one takes the motor bike why get on the bus in this traffic? So the busses were moving around Bali with no one to occupy them, go figure! Logically two things come to mind here, either the local government is slightly disorganized or a high political official has a cousin that sells busses.

Just as we got to our hotel we began our bed routine, first brushing our teeth sometimes a quick shower and sometimes a slow shower together, then we would just laid in bed watching a movie and enjoying each others company as we always do, holding hands with an occasional hug and kiss, words were irrelevant as we felt the same thing, only a glance in each others eyes was enough to read each others thoughts, we were in perfect harmony and communication together.

In general I am noticing today that people are approaching a period of time when relationships are ready to go through a major redesign. The current situation isn't working, and people are unsatisfied in love; people just don't know how to make relationships work, and so when systems break-down, that's when they change. I believe that is what's happening in the area of intimate partnership and God is using the break-down which is forcing us to move towards conscious love, which is a romantic relationship in which both partners feel committed to a sense of purpose, and that purpose is growth, individual growth and collective growth as a couple. Growth in understanding, is how God's love works with us.

As of now, most people get into relationships to satisfy their own personal needs. This might work for a few years, but eventually the relationship fails, and people end up unsatisfied as a result. But when two people come together with the intention of growth, the relationship strives towards something much greater than gratification. The partnership becomes a journey of evolution, and the two individuals have an opportunity to expand more than they could alone, and deep satisfaction and long-term fulfillment arise as a result. The reality is, ONLY GOD GIVES, and we're here to grow, spiritually, physically, mentally and emotionally, and when growth stops, we automatically feel like something's gone wrong, and because it has, because without God there is no growth, and with out growth we are not fulfilling our soul's purpose.

My *beloved lady* and I have become a conscious couple fiercely committed to being the embodiment of love. We love to communicate with each other and not just hear to respond but listen to communicate, and through our devotion to God first and practice, love shows up in our lives and in our relationship in ways we have never imagined before. We give God glory for His precious teaching.

On the 30th of May 2024 we checked out of the hotel and made our way by taxi service to the airport which should be noted that a twenty minute distance due to the traffic was done is one hour, never the less we arrived on time and parted this time around with gratitude to God and satisfaction to our own destinations, *my beloved lady* in Jakarta Indonesia and me back in Belgrade Serbia. This time we were filled with an anticipation that God will make a way for us to live under one roof, because we felt and confessed before God, man and each other that we were ready to live together, so now we were patiently waiting for Him and trusted His timing to choose and give us a house, and at His appointed place.

> Psalm 127:1 *Except the Lord build the house, they labour in vain that build it:* . . .

No one can place a sky scraper on a two story building foundation, it will not hold the weight, it will surely collapse causing great damage. No one can add new wine in old wine skins, because when fermentation occurs the old wine skin will burst and the new wine will spill out. This thinking leads to bondage in debt and foreclosure. In life there is a need first for inner transformation to be able to hold the outer reformation together, its a learning process then a doing, besides we all know that slow success builds character, fast success builds ego.

In life there is a need first for inner transformation to be able to hold the outer reformation together

Chapter 7

Money, matters!

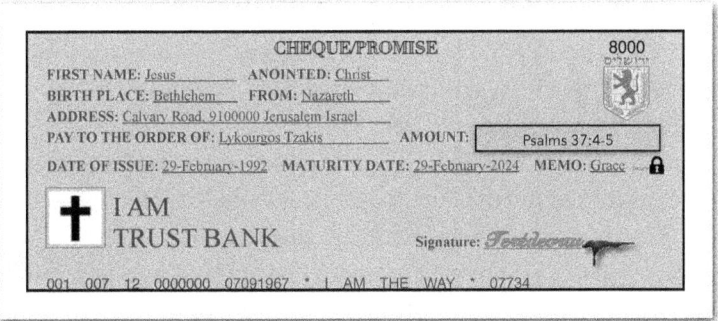

My beloved lady's favorite subject, like all or most men and women out there, we simply look at it from a different point of view, however God knows our hearts, our fears and insecurities, and motivation. Money does matter, too much of it can be as much of a problem as also lack of it, which was the reason for my ex-wife divorcing me in the first place, therefore we look to God and rely on a healthy balance and approach, to this touchy subject, that people need a special healthy teaching on, that unfortunately we also do not have in our circles.

In God's appointed timing my business partner and I after years of moulding our characters, healing our hearts and increasing us in wisdom, knowledge and understanding in order to meet and stand before the right people. We were guided by the Spirit to trust Jesus and initially exit the safety of our boat and look to Jesus only (Matthew 14:25–29), thus moving us in a different direction, and being fed spiritually, differently with strong meat. No questions asked we obeyed following Him once again through trials and tribulations (clipping of the vine), thus making us wiser, stronger, sensitive to hearing Him, while moving to another level of trusting Him even more, as He liberated us from our worst fears. You see a true measure of a person's faith, is not just the first step of their faith journey, but the subsequent steps taken thereafter.

> Matthew 6:33 *But seek ye first the kingdom of God, and his righteousness; and all these things shall be added unto you.*

Seeking the Kingdom of God involves a reorientation of our values and goals, its an inward change. Now Jesus is telling us a multiple of things here as well, He is revealing to us the secret of a successful life. He is telling us not to worry He can be trusted to take care of our needs when focusing our eyes on Him. By seeking the Kingdom of God and allowing the Holy Spirit to fill us and teach us, we slowly grow in wisdom knowledge and understanding of not only to do His work (inner transformation) but also HOW TO ACHIVE OUR PURPOSE that He implanted in us, (outer reformation), but with His ways, not our fantasy and imaginative ways that lead no where. He is the ancients of days and He knows how we as individuals and everything in the world works perfectly.

In a few months time and more fruit produced, the manifestation of His financial blessings slowly were taking physical form, first by blessing *my beloved lady* and I exactly on our one year wedding anniversary (11/06/2024). To be honest I prayed to God the previous day and asked if He wills to present us with a special wedding anniversary gift, for our future, the truth is we needed money, so when our colleague sent us the investors airline ticket issued for the eleventh of June, we immediately knew that Gods providence manifested His love, grace and mercy. The investor through our network found us and came all the way from the U.S.

to Belgrade Serbia in need of our well set up banking facility and services we provide, thus providing us with such assets that helped our company's business activities grow. Whereafter we started approaching and attracting much bigger wallets to do business with, and one thing led to another, until finally we got enough finance in order to establish a steady business, with solid steady income, and finally our lives permanently together.

On September 1st 2024, we were approached by certain government civil servants to purchase land available in Belgrade Serbia at a very…VERY cheap price per square meter, with the only obligation to only to slide something their way, and so being excited because we were ready to act and by what God was bringing our way, we immediately took this unique Real-Estate opportunity to buy and develop and manage all available real estate assets we could get our hands on, one being the planning of *the development of our own church building,* that we have been praying for. In His appointed time God gave us our hearts desire which we had been praying for many years, and this happened at a time where cash was very hard to come by.

> Proverbs 16:9 *A man's heart deviseth his way: but the Lord directeth his steps.*

God showed His awesome sovereignty, by giving us power and authority to gain wealth on earth, whereas naturally after that our business took off to a new level, we established our own offices and warehouse, adding various stock for buyers to immediately purchase. Things were on a roll and we grew in no time at all, from a company making thousands of Euros to a company making and earning millions of Euros.

The Bible contains roughly five hundred verses on prayer and faith, and in the Gospels of Matthew, Mark and Luke its estimated that one out of six verses deal somehow with money. Of the twenty nine (29) parables that Jesus told, sixteen (16) deal with the person and their money, that means that approximately forty percent of Jesus' parables deal with money. The Bible has more than two thousand (2000) verses on money. Jesus taught more on the topic of money and possessions than all of His teachings on Heaven and hell combined, so it is obvious the Bible has a lot to say about wealth and giving. A significant portion of our life will revolve around earning, saving, giving, and spending money. So our relationship with money isn't something we can just brush aside as unspiritual or unnecessary. In short, money is a medium of exchange. What we need to know about money Bible verses or not, money is amoral, neutral, money simply doesn't have a life, and it cannot act on its own, it cannot do good deeds, and it cannot commit crimes. Basically, money is neither good or bad, money can only do what you tell it to do, therefore money is not the root of all evil.

1 Tim. 6:10 *But the love of money is the root of all evil,* . . .

So the *love of money* is the root of all evil. Many verses in the Bible talk about money, because there's a direct correlation between the way we handle our money and our faith. When it comes to money, we will either worship wealth or worship with our wealth. There's a big difference between the two and thus we need to constantly monitor our heart.

*We need to learn how to think
right before we can live right*

My next move was to invite *my beloved lady* to come to Belgrade Serbia, and on her arrival when I saw her I was overwhelmed with joy, and feeling how poor I was without her all this time, she was also filled with joy even more so when I had already purchased our own house, and a new car, I just adore looking at her beautiful smile, knowing she is happy and feeling secure, besides being together is what we both always wanted and longed for. My next and final mission is to live my life introducing to *my beloved lady* practically the greatest love of all, for that is the greatest gift I can ever give to her. Perfect love (AGAPI) is explained in (1 Corinthians 13:4–8), this is the perfect love that we are not only called to exercise with one another but this is the love that God expresses

Himself towards us and this same love is what we learn from Him as the ultimate example that we should express back to God.

Truth be told, I really hate religion in any form followed by traditionalism, legalism, extreme liberalism vine philosophy and worse peoples believe–ism (no works of faith), well simply because it messes people up, in ways many of us can not even imagine. Religion was used in the early times as a way for smart educated people to manipulate and control the simple not so smart and uneducated people. We need to be very careful, what other books we read and who we listen to, and always we need to be on high alert. However we also need to know that: *With discernment comes division.* A person seeking wisdom knowledge and understanding, to be able to judge well, or righteously, must be willing to suffer the effects of this division. It will divide not only believer form unbeliever, but it may also divide a discerning believer from one who is undiscerning, it will separate the mature and wise from the Immature and foolish. Sometimes people don't want to hear the truth because they don't want their illusions destroyed. Or worse: You can give a person knowledge, but you can't make them think, because some people want to remain fools, only because the truth requires change.

Worship is fear towards God not by the precepts of men

King Saul was religious, no heart, no intimate relationship with God, so when he sinned he made excuses, blaming others, and got fired from his job from God. King David on the other hand sinned also and worse off than Saul, but he had a heart for God, no excuses, repented because he loved God, and therefore was forgiven by God, remember that people when the *judging* and *gossip* starts. It is about the attitude of our heart and not the external rituals and observances that we think are so important. Only the word of God is the compass that can guide us in life's journey, and we need to study it closely so nobody can dictate fairy tales to us, misleading and binding us with vain words and theories, and apart from all that no man is mandated by God to judge another man, so let us relax and let God run the universe.

The fact is that nobody loves us as much as Jesus does, He left His throne of comfort, with out a second thought, and despite the knowledge of His death He still came, His will with out a reasonable doubt to our benefit, He is the real hero, my hero!

Finally the happy end that everyone is looking for in this beautiful and true love story. So because God truly loves us, and cares for us, and because we placed our trust in Him, and in His timing, *my beloved lady,* whereas by her own free will and choice now *beloved sister in Christ,* and I *His servant,* live a simple and quiet life, united under God. Free, Healthy, Wealthy and Happily ever after, enjoying life at its fullest, for *life is for the living!*

Never be afraid of an unknown future
You are in the hands of a well known God

The End

Epilogue

DEARLY BELOVED THIS IS our Love Story, our personal romantic testimony between God and us, all this and much more that one book alone can not contain, orchestrated by God that loves and cares for us with precise dates and with a sufficient number of witnesses that can testify all is true concerning this romantic love story. I also wanted the details written as a record to remind *my beloved lady* and I whenever we read through it to give God, glory honor and praise for all that we have, and all He has knitted so perfectly together to give us happiness, and satisfaction, also *words not written are easily forgotten.*

    A bit of warning to those reading and understanding something different of that which I am trying to teach here, this love story is in no means a formula as an excuse for liberal sexual intercourse and a get rich scheme, for everyone to adapt and follow, "*not so*", this is personal. God almighty, omniscient, omnipresent behind the scenes reserves the right to speak to anyone at any time with what ever means He wants with. Those who do not wait or acknowledge upon God and rush into marriage contract, only to invite God as a guest in their wedding ceremony for the wrong reasons will not benefit anything, and/or worse, the wrong motivation could have the opposite results, of what one might expect for *God knows the hearts of man, and can not be fooled.* To seek His face is not the same thing as approaching him on a basis of need. Seeking His face speaks of being with Him, spending time with Him, knowing Him, his ways, his thoughts. Therefore *seek the giver whole heartedly, not the gift.*

Love Story

Jesus is the ultimate reward

There are some eternal principles that govern everything in life. *Difficult times shape strong men, strong men create good times, good times produce weak men, and weak men create hard times. Easy gain and comfort in every country produces parasites and not fighters of life.*

We all have said one time or another that we would love a bit of change in our lives, we do not like it to be so monotonous and boring all the time. However what people really mean is, they love change as long as they initiate that change, they do not like when someone else initiate it and changes our comfort in the process, because we do not want to get out of our comfort zone. Most of us have Junk in our lives, and we are used to this, and God starts to shake things up, so before we shake our fist to God, let us stop and think, that God might have something better for us down the road, therefore storms change comfort.

Everything that I have ever been through trials and sufferings, was permitted by God, the fire purified me, and made me dependent on Him as I slowly discovered my strengths, I feared less and trusted Him more, while opening my eyes to wisdom knowledge and understanding and values I knew not, I was taught to love and understand His love for me, I am intrigued by the way He loves me, to Him I have value and I just can not get enough of Him, so much so I discovered how poor I was without Him. I discovered places I knew not, and ways I had thought not of, and along the way I discovered good people, that helped me not only to fulfill that which He implanted inside my heart, but they too became saved by the pureness of my hands, and all of this simply because He was preparing me to receive and keep that which I prayed for, in His perfect time, by His perfect will.

The end is more important than the beginning

About the Author

LYKOURGOS TZAKIS WAS BORN September 07 1967 in Athens Greece, and originated from an Ionian Island called Kefallonia. He moved to the U.S. at an early age where he lived during the most sensitive years of his teenage youth. Where only just about sixteen years old, parents decide to move back to Kefallonia Greece where he finished the remaining two years of high school and later graduated from a private music academy. It was in Kefallonia Greece in 1990 that he gave his heart to the Lord Jesus Christ and was instantly healed by Krohns Disease.

Lykourgos Tzakis is a member of the Hellenic Evangelical Church in Athens Greece where he served from 2000 to 2009 as the first drummer, assisting Mr. Bill Baldwin to change the traditional religious status to a up to date praise and worship system that led to growth with young people attending the Sunday service, in short time other modern musical instruments were added enriching praise & worship and recording their first CD "*Στο Σταυρό*" (on the cross) with one of his hymns "*Μεγας Είσαι Κύριε Θεέ*" (Great You are). In 2015 he relocated his business in Belgrade Serbia with a partner and became a member of the International Cristian Fellowship (ICF).

Lykourgos Tzakis Interacts on a daily business basis with various people of a different ethnicity, culture and background thus perceiving the need for a simple up to date and practical teaching of Scripture. So in 2020 he dedicated in a depth study of the New Testament, historical & cultural research, analyzing the correct and full meaning of the ancient Greek words that are essential in explaining Scripture (The New Testament) with commentary, practical examples and testimonies teaching and spreading a fresh up to date and practical Gospel all over the world. Simultaneously tearing down false doctrine that arise due to assumptions, vain philosophies and lack of knowledge. Much later formed and founded "*The Way Ministries*," where his Bible Study Guides simply and practically explain and teach all people various as well as specific theological subjects, on how to put in practical supplement all that we read in our daily lives.

All published material of the New Testament are recorded separately as a small practical hand book either to follow up on, or to be used to teach others with, for the furtherance of the Gospel.

Eagles fly and nest high!

www.ingramcontent.com/pod-product-compliance
Lightning Source LLC
Chambersburg PA
CBHW071747040426
42446CB00012B/2493